The Minimalist Guide To Prepping: Being Prepared Without Being Obsessed

Introduction

I want to thank you for reading this book, *"The Minimalist Guide To Prepping: Being Prepared Without Being Obsessed"*.

This book contains simple techniques to be prep in your spare time.

Too many Preppers spend far too much time prepping, sacrificing these calm times preparing for the coming "Doomsday".

It's time to relax.

Just do what is absolutely necessary and go on with your life.

Thanks again for reading this book, I know you'll enjoy it!

What To Have On Hand

Commercialized prepping involves buying loads of stuff. This means filling an overgrown storage unit with enough food that can feed a small community. That's just plain expensive, too much work, and in some states, downright illegal (anti hoarding laws).

The problem with hoarding is, When The Shit Hits The Fan (WTSHTF), no matter how protected you think you are, there is always someone else who is crazy enough to try and take it away from you. Moreover, you, just sitting there, with your hoard of goods, is an open invitation for marauders.

The minimalist prepper is more realistic. He knows that a doomsday scenario is unlikely, but is wise enough to prepare, just in case. He understands that mobility, variety, and adequate training are the keys to survival. Simply put, you need your food and water stores to fit whatever vehicle you might have. The same can even be trimmed some more into personal backpacks of survival essentials.

Back to the Basics (60:30:9:1)

You want to have something that will last you a week, or a month at most. The equation is simple; 60% water; 30% food; 9% clothing and 1% medicine. Think of it as emergency rations for when a storm hits.

What Not to Buy

Before we discuss in detail the things you will need, we must first discuss things you will not need. To wit:

- Commercial prepper foodstuff. These are just plain expensive. Most of the stuff included is just overpriced.
- Celebrity Survival Kits: It's crazy! No self-respecting honest to goodness prepper would be caught in the woods with Bear, what's his name's brand of survival kits. They'd rather have a machete instead.
- Tons of stuff: you don't need to buy 50-gallon PET drums for water. You don't need to buy commercially packed grains. You don't need an arsenal fit for an army.

What to Buy

Now we finally get to the essentials. Remember, this is only a blueprint. When in doubt, go back to the equation 60:30:9:1.

Water

You don't need to buy bottled water. You can, but you don't have to. Tap water will do. But, of course this presupposes that you have checked your local water system and made sure it is safe to drink and store. Also, you need to understand that self-stored water need to be used 3 to 6 months from the time it has been stored. In the worst of times, 1 to 2 years is okay. But it would be best to boil it before drinking.

Water Containers

You will need sturdy, yet lightweight water containers; of different sizes, and made from different materials. Most of which you will be using at home anyway. Others you will be buying specifically for preparedness, and in preparation for hobbies associated with prepping i.e. hiking.

Glass containers

The problem with these containers is that they are heavy and breakable. A couple of glass containers can prove useful, but majority of your containers should be made of PET.

Steel Containers

You need at least one steel container, preferably stainless steel. Don't buy the enameled types or those with plastic additions. This way you can place it on top of hot coals or hang it over a fire. Heck, if you are a hiking geek, then you probably have a titanium one at that. Whichever one you choose, it should at least be able to contain 8 ounces of fluids, and has a large mouth and a re-sealable lid.

PET Grade

Granted, there is much ado over nothing, about the different PET grades (recycling number). But you might as well err on the side of caution and use recycling codes 2, 4, and 5. Avoid the codes 3 and 7. The important thing is that the containers are clean and have only been used to store water.

You want to have several containers, some of which are of different sizes. Personally the author has:

- 1 x 5 gallon PET container per person in the family
- 3 x 8 to 16 ounce PET container per person in the family
- 1 x 3 to 5 liter hydration bladder per person in the family
- 1 x stainless steel canteen, preferably wide mouthed.

Water Purification

When the shit hits the fan, the minimalist prepper scavenges for water: in which case it might not always be immediately drinkable. As such, you are required to have some sort of water purification method.

Let us assume that you found a murky water source i.e. a pond. It goes without saying that you should boil the water first. That's what your wide mouth canteen is for. But before that, you would do well to filter the murky water so that it's clean.

Below is a relatively inexpensive DIY type filtration device. You will need:

- 1 twist open body PET container i.e. Copco 16.9 ounce hydra bottle)
- Several cotton balls or 2 wads of cotton fabric
- Sand
- Limestone pebbles
- Charcoal pebbles (not powdery but hard grits)

Unscrew the hydra bottle. Take the top portion and turn it upside-down. Place some cotton balls or a wad of cotton fabric to plug the small hole underneath. Add an inch of limestone pebbles; followed by an inch of sand; then another inch of charcoal. Top it off with cotton or another wad of cotton fabric. Gently compact the mix, taking care not to disturb the layers.

Now lay the top portion on top of the lower portion of the hydra bottle. This will serve as a handy filtration and catchment device.

Tip: it would be best if you keep each filtration layer inside cotton pouches that follows the contours of the top part of the hydration bottle. All you need is some basic sewing knowledge. This way you can easily reuse it for a very long time.

Water Tabs

You can also buy several water purification tablets like Troclosene sodium (Aquatabs). This will allow you to purify your drinking water on the go. In any case these are very cheap. Just make sure to follow the instructions. Some tabs dilute 1 tablet per 1 liter, other dilute 1 tablet per 20 liters.

Emergency Purification

You might as well know that, in the worst of times, you can use iodine or chlorine bleach to purify water. You only do this if boiling the water is not possible. First, make sure you are using chlorine bleach or iodine (2% iodine with 47% alcohol), not soap laced or scented chlorine or feminine wash iodine. Second, filter cloudy or murky water first.

- Chlorine bleach: 8 drops per gallon of water
- Iodine: 5 drops per quart for clear water. 8 drops per quart for cloudy water

Food

You want food that is ready to eat. It would also be best to buy food that can be mixed together and still taste good i.e. spam with pork and beans. There is much debate about dehydrated packs vs. canned goods vs. tetra packed food. The author is of the opinion that you should use whatever is available in your location for a cheap price. Also, you might as well keep a variety of food, but minimize on dehydrated food. This is because you will be required to use precious water or even cook the same over a fire.

Another consideration is weight. Canned foods will always be heavier than tetra packed or dehydrated foods. If you must buy canned foods, select aluminum type cans that you can repurpose. Oh, and easy open cans are preferred, but the minimalist prepper can make do with whatever is in the pantry WTSHTF.

For example:

- Spam containers can be used as your individual serving dish. You can also collect water with it.
- Libby's sausage can or the like can be re-purposed as an alcohol stove.
- Cans of peaches can be used as traps for catching small animals.

Personally, the author keeps the pantry fully stocked with assorted goods. To be clear, primary consideration is always stuff eaten on a regular basis. Secondary consideration is, WTSHTF scenario.

Tip: when purchasing canned goods, be selective of the expiration dates. You want to buy goods that keep longer, just in case you need to bunker down. Do not buy dented, bloated, and rusty cans.

Below are the canned goods the author personally stocks up on:

- Spam lite (low sodium means less thirst)
- Pork and beans
- Sausages
- Pineapples
- Peaches
- String beans
- Tuna
- Sardines

Grains and other edibles

Aside from canned goods, you should also be stocked on grains. More importantly, you should be familiar with how to cook it. Would you believe some preppers stock up on tons of rice but have absolutely no idea how to cook it?

It is very much recommended to stock up on grains that are high on carbohydrates, fibers, and keep long. For example:

- Oats
- Rice
- Corn (whole kernels and ground)
- Wheat (whole and in flour form)

Clothing

WTSHTF, the right type of clothing is essential. The best thing you can do is keep an extra set of shirts, pants, socks, sandals, jacket, and a blanket. Any material will do. But you need to consider the weather of your location. Also, clothes made from dry fit materials are best because they are light and dry fast.

To save space in your backpack, you want to be wearing layers of clothing. The author prefers: a sleeveless dry fit shirt; on top of a long sleeved dry fit shirt; a pair of sturdy khaki cargo pants; mid cut boots; and a jacket wrapped around the waist. The best colors to wear are dull colors. This way you do not attract unnecessary attention. Of course, it is also a good idea to have a colorful bandana tucked away, to signal for help.

Tip: extra-large garbage bags can be used as a poncho, shelter or additional carrying compartment.

Medicine

You only carry 1% medicine so you better pack effectively and efficiently. You want to cover all your bases. This 1% does not include any specific medication you need to take on a regular basis. For example:

- Antibiotic/antibacterial meds

- Antiseptic i.e. iodine
- Pain relievers
- Cough medicine (a cough can give away your hiding spot)
- Bandages
- Cotton and gauze
- Fever and flu medicine
- Sutures

Just like when buying food, always be wary of expiration dates when buying your medicine.

Live Protein

Forget about pork and beef. WTSHTF, you want live meat to be easy to carry and transport. You also want them to breed like, well like rabbits. You might as well get used to taking care of some chickens and rabbits in your backyard. Other contenders include but are not limited to:

- Guinea pig
- Grasshoppers
- Earthworms
- Snails
- Frogs

Summary

To sum things up: on hand items must include the following:

- Water (tap water will do)
- Different sized PET water containers and 1 wide mount stainless steel canteen.

- Homemade filtration device
- Water purification tablets, tincture of iodine, and unscented chlorine bleach
- Canned goods
- Various grains
- Clothes
- Medicine
- Small livestock (you hand carry)

Chapter 2

The Bug Out Bag

You will be preparing 2 types of bug out bags per individual. The first is the basic bag that allows you to drink, eat and be relatively comfortable for at least 1 week.

Bug Out Backpack

The ideal bug out pack is a hiking backpack, probably around 3o to 60 liters in capacity. The rule is, each person must not carry more than 30% of his/her body weight. If you have small children, any of their backpacks will do. Yes, everyone has to contribute with the load as well. The only exceptions are children of tender years (below 4), a handicapped individual who cannot possibly carry any load, the sick and individuals of advanced years (70 and up)

This is a minimalist eBook, so why should you buy a hiking backpack? Simple, it's a necessary gear. This is especially true because, one of the necessary skills a minimalist prepper must learn is how to hike in the woods. Remember, you will be trading off goods for experience and training, but there are some items you just need to have.

The contents of your bug out bag were already provided in the first chapter. You need one week's supply mind you! How to correctly ration will be discussed in the next chapter.

Stand Alone vs. Item Distribution

Generally, each backpack should contain survival essentials. Of course, bigger and more able members of the household, need to carry more in terms of food, water, medicine, and even shelter i.e. cook set, tent, etc.

Tip: play with different scenarios. This way you are able to cope with different situations that might arise.

For example: one family member gets injured and cannot carry an item. How would you redistribute the pack content? The worst you can do is to leave the pack behind. You need to provide some extra space in each backpack, in order to redistribute the contents of the injured person's pack, and maybe even some scavenged stuff.

Get Home Kit

The purpose of your get home kit is to allow you to go back home and get to your bug out bag. The usual scenario is: you are at the office, school, buying groceries, or on the road, and TSHTF. The highway gets clogged and there's panic everywhere. You need to ditch your car and get back home. Any backpack will do.

You will need:

- Shoes: you need a comfy and sturdy pair that will allow you to jog and run home. A pair of hiking or jogging shoes works great. When it's wintertime, add a pair of traction soles to your get home kit.
- Water: You want to have at least 500 ml (16 ounces). If you can manage 1 liter, that's better.

- Clothing: change the clothing on your get home kit based on the season. If it's summer, dry fit clothes will do. If it's winter, then fleece is a good idea.
- Food: trail mix will do.
- Bicycle: if you've got a folding bike, might as well lug it around.

Chapter 3

Skills To Learn Between Now And The Apocalypse

The minimalist prepper does not over react. When it comes to training, you want to take things 1 step at a time. Think of your training as level based. You first complete level 1 sets of skills, then move up to level 2, then level 3. This allows you to learn several important skills in the least amount of time. After you've completed a cycle of skills, then you can go back to the first, and then increase your knowledge base.

Nutrition and Rationing

Under normal circumstances, you call this a balanced diet. WTSHTF, you call this intelligent rationing. You need to know how much and what type of food, plus water, each individual in your family needs.

According to studies, the human body requires 2,000 to 2,400 calories a day in order to maintain his/her body weight. In a survival situation, with proper rations, you can cut that in half. In the worst of times, you can even go as low as 500 to 800 calories.

To put that into perspective, 2,400 is a generous lunch sized serving of pasta, veggies, and poultry. 1,200 calories is a diet-sized meal. 500 calories is roughly 1 half of a regular-sized burger.

As such, it is very important to know how to count calories. There are websites that allow you to count calories. Heck, there are even mobile apps for that. By practicing now, you can eventually get a rough estimate WTSHTF. A more scientific approach would be to write down how many calories each meal or snack amounts to: For example:

1. 1 cup oats (234 grams) = 158 calories
2. 1 can string beans (100 grams) = 31 calories
3. 1 cup pork and beans (234 grams) = 268 calories
4. 1 can of tuna (100 grams) = 184 calories
5. 1 can of spam lite (100 grams) = 191 calories
6. 1 cup of peaches (100 grams) = 39 calories
7. Saltine (soda) crackers (1 piece) = 13 calories

Nutrition Level

Counting calories is not enough. Let's face it; the minimalist prepper will be hard pressed to maintain a balance diet. What you can do is make sure that you at least eat 1 diet-sized meal a day. Every day, you need to vary your food intake so that you have fiber, carbohydrates, fat, protein, etc.

Calories In vs. Calories Out

"Calories in", refers to the amount and quality of food that you eat. "Calories out", refers to the physical exertion that you perform. Always remember, the more Calories you burn, the more calories you need to eat. Tip: WTSHTF, avoid unnecessary movements to save on calories.

Prioritize individuals who exert more effort i.e. scavenge, hunt, etc.

Weight In

As early as now, you want to weigh yourself. Is this the weight you want to maintain? Are you overweight or underweight? The minimalist prepper needs to be in the best shape of his life. This allows him to eat the least amount of food, in order to maintain his weight and adequately answer to his nutritional needs.

Hiking and Survival Essentials

The minimalist prepper has been there and done that! Well, not exactly in a WTSHTF scenario, but very near it. The only way to simulate this is by hiking and camping in the outdoors. Chances are, on your first hike, you'll bring too much and immediately realize that carrying too much is the wrong thing to do. On your second hike, you'll probably under pack and realize, that's not right either. On your third, maybe fourth hike, if you are smart, you'll have found the middle ground between packing light and staying comfy. Below are a few hiking essentials to remember:

- Different seasons require different gear and have different challenges. You need to be an ALL season hiker, if you want to survive the worst of times.
- Multi day hikes are best. Of course you will start with day hikes. You eventually progress to 2, 3, 4, 5, or more days outdoors.
- Discomfort is unavoidable. Pitying yourself is optional.

Shelter

WTSHTF, you need to be prepared to evacuate your home and travel long distances on foot. As such, you need to have some form of shelter. This can be something you bring with you i.e. tent, tarp, sleeping bag, hammock, etc. Or this can be something you build using skills you have acquired.

Buy a tent or tarp with muted colors and fits your environment. For example: you want to buy a tarp with green on one side and white on the other. This way you can use it during the summers and winters.

What is better: A readymade tent i.e. dome, tadpole or a tarp that can be made into a tent? The answer depends. First, you utilize what you have. If you don't have a tent readymade, or manufactured tent, chances are you have a tarp. Other considerations include:

- Privacy: a manufactured tent usually allows you some level of privacy.
- Alertness: on the negative side, privacy can also lead to you, not being able to see and hear what is going on outside.
- Weight: a tarp is usually lighter, since it has fewer folds, seams, and poles.
- Ease of use: A tent is easier to erect but longer to disassemble and pack.
- Weather: if you live in a place with extreme temperatures, you want to adapt your shelter to that. For example: if you live in a place with very warm weather, then a tarp might be cooler. If you live in a place where it gets cold or even snows a lot, a closed tent might be better.

Tip: a hiker usually has both a tent and a tarp. You can use your tarp as additional shelter or as a footprint as an added insulation from the ground. That is, if you can carry the load. Again, the more experienced as a hiker you are, the better you are at living while on the road or as a nomad.

Nomadic Cultivation

A minimalist prepper knows his plants. He can grow edible plants, identify medicinal herbs, and knows how to camouflage them to keep them away from prying eyes. Forget about a standalone sustainable garden in a farm or on your backyard. That's just an open invitation for marauders. You'd be lucky if they'd be content with stealing the plants you've cultivated.

The better approach is to cultivate edible and medical plants on small patches i.e. roadside, in between tall grasses. This is easier to camouflage and overlook. The best way to go about this is to be familiar with your surroundings.

- What edible and medicinal plants are endemic to your location and within a 50-mile radius of you?
- Can you identify places where these grow naturally?
- Can you look for out of the way locations where you can cultivate edible plant life?
- Can you camouflage the same, to minimize the risk of discovery?
- Can you get back and leave the vicinity without being seen, or without leaving signs of your presence?

Livestock Rearing

The minimalist prepper needs protein and meat. He must know what are edible and what are not edible. He must not be picky with what he eats. As such, you need to know how to trap, rear, and slaughter small game like rodents, lizards, birds, insects, fish, crustaceans, etc. This isn't a game! This is survival. So as early as now, learn how to slaughter and gut a mouse, guinea pig, rabbit, small birds, etc. Eat as much of the flesh as you can. Heck, insects are fair game too! Just make sure you know how to safely prepare your meat before eating it, and which insects are safe to eat.

Foraging for Food and Water

The minimalist prepper only has a week of food and water stored, maybe 1 month at most. That is why, it is important to save what you have stored and continually look for other sources of food and water. This is also an outdoor skill that can be taught to clueless city slickers. All you need to do is to pay attention. Different situations call for different approaches. Remember, every drop counts. Below are a few that you can learn from hiking and outdoor classes:

- *The city*: You will have to forage for food and water from abandoned houses, cars, buildings, etc. Remember, there might not be water on the tap. But there might be water on the pipes. First, you need to do is close all the faucets in the facility. Second, open the topmost faucet. Third, go to the lowest faucet and open it. If there is any water left, gravity should send it to you and your waiting container!

Tip: when foraging for food. Look for best before and expiration dates. In case of the former, the date is only indicative of freshness. As long as 6 months to 1 year has not lapsed, it should still be good to go. In case of the later, usually, manufacturers allow a 3-month buffer, before it actually expires. But that still depends on how it was stored.

- **The forest**: Water is not always at the lowest point. You need to look for signs of water. Your first clue is vegetation. Look for greener and fuller trees or grass. Your second clue is animal droppings. The more animal droppings there are, the nearer you are to water. After pinpointing the first two, you can then travel downwards. When you do come into a riverbed, you might find that it's dried up. Not to worry, look for the lowest point and dig. Also, look for a point where the soil meets a rock formation dig there as well.
- **Desert conditions**: Plant life will guide you to sources of water. You can also suck the moisture out of plants like cactus. Use the process of water condensation to purify any murky liquids or even your own urine. All you need to do is place the fluid in a clear container. Now place a thin membrane in between the container and the sun. Place it

in a diagonal position so that any moisture collected will travel down, and onto a shaded collection area. The most basic set up requires 2 pet bottles, a plastic sheet, a few sticks, or stones, and lots of patience.

- ***River and Lakes***: You have two concerns here: first is filtration, second is safety. Strategically speaking, open sources of water are great places for an ambush. Always be wary of open sources of water. Check the perimeter, before collecting water. If you are in a tight spot, always leave a spotter or several spotters, to make sure that you can deflect any ambushes.

Rain Water

To any prepper, the rain is a blessing. But you need to be set up so you can collect as much water as you can. The best way to do this is via underground water catchment. No need to get fancy. Use what you have to catch as much water as possible. You can even create a makeshift pond by digging a hole in the ground and placing a black plastic bag on top of the hole. Just make sure there are no leaks.

Storage Concerns

What do you do with the water you collected? Well, you keep as much on your person as possible. You hide your surplus in several locations in small caches. This way, if one cache is compromised, you still have other stores to go to. Most preppers are trained to store their water via:

- *Digging a hole and burying it.* This is a good idea if the environment is hot and arid. By burying it underground, you minimize loss due to condensation. But be careful that there isn't any visible signs, otherwise, some other curious person, might just dig it up.

- *Storing it in out of the way locations.* This is good for places with plenty of junk.

Building a Fire

Fire is necessary for warmth, for boiling water, and for cooking food. WTSHTF, you need to be an expert at building a fire, using several methodologies. It helps if you carry your own flint and matches with you. But you also need to know how to build a fire using wood-to-wood friction.

Another important skill is to build your fire so that it is not visible from several yards away. The trick is to build it low and small. Also, you want to use a fuel source that generates the least smell.

Keeping Clean

This is not only for vanity's sake. Clean, means less prone to infection. In the woods, it also means a hungry bear won't try to eat you for lunch. And, it's good for morale. Just think of how bad it will smell inside a small shelter, if you don't keep yourself clean. There is also the comfort factor.

To be clear, WTSHTF, you don't want to be wasting resources. But you can utilize plants and herbs in order to sanitize yourself. Certain herbs and leaves can be crushed and applied poultice like to your skin, teeth and gums. Of course, you want to make sure you are actually using safe leaves and not poisonous one's like poison ivy.

- Basil is not just used for cooking you can also use it as a kind of toothpaste to keep your mouth clean and your breath fresh.
- Citronella leaves can keep away the insects and clean your skin
- Lavender leaves and flowers can be crushed to sanitize and freshen you up.

Advanced First Aid

Basic first aid will not be enough. Let's face it; even a grade-schooler knows how to put on a Band-Aid. What you need is advanced first aid i.e. how to sew horrible gashes; how to mend broken bones; how to cauterize wounds; even, the basics of amputation. Remember, you will have very limited supplies. So you need to improvise as well. The best place to learn this is also in hiking and survival courses. Granted, you may not be able to apply these skills. But knowing the basics can save yours and another person's life.

Fortification vs. Camouflage

A rich prepper can fortify a remote area and keep himself safe. A minimalist prepper makes his home base look abandoned, or lives a nomadic life. The author is of the opinion that, if you do find a place you can fortify and keep hidden from view, go for it. But to be realistic, fortifying a home, or even your basement can only get you so far. But, if you plan to do so, then at least have an exit strategy on hand.

Keeping Morale Up

Last, but not the least, you need to know how to keep from going insane. WTSHTF you've just gone from a comfortable lifestyle to subsistence living. You'll be bored, depressed, tired. All sorts of negative emotions will pop up. You need to keep yourself motivated. The author suggests having a short-term goal in mind. When you meet that goal, you reward yourself, maybe with a sip of water, a small bite to eat, or even a hug from your companion.

Chapter 4

Self Defense

WTSHTF, you may be left to your own devices. There won't be any police to regulate human behavior. Heck, there might not even be any form of government whatsoever. There are several ways to go about this. To be clear, your first priority is always to evade. Only when you cannot do so, do you resort to defense, and offense.

Fitness and Mindset

You and your group must be able to rely on each other. Every member must be as fit as possible. Of course, you don't forsake the injured or the elderly. You become fit, in order to better protect each other. In this regard, nothing beats jogging as a fitness base. It's inexpensive, fun, and can be done with minimal training. You also expect to be walking and even jogging a lot, either as a form of travel, or evasion.

Camouflage and Evasion

WTSHTF, you want to keep to yourself as much as possible. This is because; you never know what others might be up to. Seriously, don't you watch The Walking Dead!? In hiking, this is called "Leave No Trace" (LNT). There are seminars for this. The same is usually related to self-defense or hunting. Essentially you:

- Make sure no one can track you back to your shelter for the night.

- No one track you when harvesting from your secret stash.

Chivalry Died A Long Time Ago

WTSHTF, your first priority is to live. That is why; you throw away the notion of fair play and chivalry. You do everything in your power and use everything within your disposal to keep you, and your family, safe. Because, you can be sure that the other person is also going to do so! That said, notice that the discussion starts with guns and move on to hand-to-hand combat. This is because; you only resort to using your fists as a last resort. For one, you might lose. Second, even if you do win, you will most likely be injured. You can't just walk into a hospital and get treated you know. Always remember: Evade, Shoot, Knife, and then Punch.

Guns and Ammo

The author has mixed feelings on this one. Personally, yours truly prefers a compound bow. It's quieter and, if aimed correctly, you can reuse the arrows. The only downside to this is it requires a lot of training to shoot a compound bow with a certain level of accuracy. There is also the fact that you will be shooting at a live target.

The author recommends hunting for big game as practice i.e. deer, elk, etc.

That said, you should know how to handle several different types of guns i.e. handguns, shotguns, rifles, etc. You don't necessarily have to own one. But WTSHTF, if you come across one, you bag it and be thankful for the added protection.

Safety First

If you do have a compound bow and/or a gun, keep it locked up. ALWAYS store the ammunition in a separate container. Make sure your gun or bow is not loaded. Check the chamber of your gun as well.

Non-Projectile Weapons

This includes but is not limited to knives, baseball bats, steel pipes, etc. As a general rule of thumb, you swing or jab fast and with as minimal wasted movement as possible. Your goal here is to create space between you and your attacker. That space can then be utilized to run or create an opening for a better attack.

The last thing you want to do is throw away your weapon. Remember; always hold your weapon gently but firmly. Don't show it off like an amateur or hold it tightly. Hold it loosely like you've done this a dozen of times before. Let the assailant know you have a weapon. If he backs off, then all is well and good; if not, then it can get ugly.

Hand to Hand

Conventional hand-to-hand combat will not do. In a real street fight, there are no rules. When you strike your opponent, you need to have the intention of maiming. The best hand-to-hand skills are those the military uses. Judo is also a good choice. This is because it teaches you how to violently slam an opponent onto the ground. And without any protective mat, that act can stun or injure someone.

Driving

Yes, driving can also be considered self-defense. This means not ordinary driving, but the ability to drive fast, change positions, reverse, and even use your vehicle as a battering ram. These skills can be learned in advanced driving classes. Heck, preppers have a special class for this.

Keeping Watch

WTSHTF, 8 hours of continuous sleep is a luxury that most cannot afford. At most, 4 hours will do. But more importantly, at least 1 person has to keep watch. Everyone must realize how important this is. If you are in a large group, you can keep watch in pairs. But be careful not to talk to each other because this will distract you.

If you are in a small group, then you need to keep alert at all times. It only takes a couple of minutes of inattention for marauders to be on top of your group.

Group Prepping

WTSHTF, you don't want to be alone. You want to be in a small, well-trained group. Now, preferably, you already know these individuals. Chances are you've trained together. This may sound harsh, but you only trust your group. Everybody else is a potential threat.

Other Training Needs

This will change depending on the situation. It would be best to have a solid base on several knowledge bases though. For example:

- *Swimming*: If you live in an area with a lot of lakes or rivers, then you need to know how to swim. This can be done for evasion or to gather food i.e. fishing.
- *Signals*: you want to communicate with someone silently or over long distances. This way you can warn someone of danger or sneak up on your prey. Think of hand signs, birdcalls, or smoke signals, or the arrangement of rocks, twig, leaves, etc.
- *Driving*: you need to know how to drive different modes of transportation. For example, you want to know how to use both a stick shift and an automatic transmission. You want to know how to ride a motorbike and a bike. You need to know how to operate a speedboat or a hovercraft even.

Chapter 5

Gold, Silver, And Bartering

WTSHTF, cash may lose its value. This is a fact, and one that has happened several times already. For example, during the great depression, a bag full of cash won't even buy you a pound of wheat. In most cases, commerce will go back to the use of precious metals and stones, or the bartering of goods.

If you have jewelry of value, keep the same safe. You can use that in a pinch. Using precious metals and stones presupposes surplus. However, let's be realistic, in the worst of times, food and water will always be the currency of choice.

This brings us back to water collection, cultivation, and rearing of small livestock. That extra bottle of water can be traded for a pound of oats or vice versa. A couple of tomatoes can be bartered for eggs. Chickens that produce meat and eggs will be worth its weight in gold. A sheep with its meat, milk, and wool, is a treasure throve.

Be Wary

If you do intend to barter, make sure no one knows where you keep your stash. Don't boast about having more. Always look like this is all you've got. Be especially wary when you travel back, after you've just bartered. You don't want anybody to follow you. Don't go straight to your campsite. You might be leading marauders there.

Have Back Up

It is best to bring someone with you. You can either move together, or have your partner standby, and out of sight. When you leave, your partner follows, this way he makes sure you are not being followed, or neutralizes the treat. Typically, you want to be a group of four. Two of you barter, the other two keeps watch for anything suspicious. This way, anybody who sees you knows you have back up. The other two keeps out of sight. You have some form of signal or a choke point.

Chapter 6

What To Tell Your Spouse And Children

Prepping, even via minimalist approach takes time and costs money. You don't tell your spouse and your kids you are preparing for doomsday. The kids might think it's cool. Your teenager might think you are a loser. Your spouse might think you're crazy or leave you. What you do tell her is that you are preparing for a disaster.

A typical example would be Hurricane Katrina. You don't want to be stuck without food and water for several days. You also bring her along on your hiking trips and seminars. This can be under the guise of a family bonding session. You can then slowly but surely wheedle your way into adding more intense training and additional gear as time passes.

Of course your spouse and kids aren't dumb. After a while, they'll figure out you are prepping for something more than an ordinary disaster. Go ahead and come out. As long as you did not go overboard with the expenses, your spouse will understand. It is for the protection of your family. Also, by then they've probably been hooked, or you at least have your basic gear.

When the Shit Hits the Fan

If disaster does strike, you need to prepare yourself for several scenarios. This includes being isolated from each other i.e. you are at work, junior is at school, your wife is at home. You need to have a system set up to make sure that all of you meet up. If your spouse and kids are game for it, you can even practice different evacuation strategies.

Assuming you've gotten together. You must be the pillar of strength for your kids. Avoid arguing, and looking lost. Assume the position of the alpha. Allow a consensus, save for the most extreme circumstances.

Tip: always keep a sense of normalcy. For example, saying grace, being thankful, eating together.

Remember, the shit has hit the fan, but it doesn't mean you should fall to pieces. In the meantime, go on with your life. Enjoy what this world has to offer.

Conclusion

Thank you again for reading this book!

I hope this book helped you sort how you need to prep!

Finally, if you enjoyed this book, then I'd like to ask you for a favor, would you be kind enough to leave a review for this book? It'd be greatly appreciated!

Thank you, and good luck prepping!

Made in the USA
San Bernardino, CA
16 May 2018